Twenty to Make

Sugar Scaries

Frances
McNaughton

Search Press

First published in Great Britain 2013

Search Press Limited
Wellwood, North Farm Road,
Tunbridge Wells, Kent TN2 3DR

Text copyright © Frances McNaughton 2013

Photographs by Vanessa Davies at
Search Press Studios

Photographs and design copyright
© Search Press Ltd 2013

ISBN: 978-1-84448-941-1

Suppliers
If you have difficulty in obtaining any of the
materials and equipment mentioned in this
book, then please visit the Search Press website
for details of suppliers: www.searchpress.com

Printed in Malaysia

Dedication
To my nephews and nieces:
Katie, Harvey, Ruby, Jack, Olivia
and Sasha.

Contents

Introduction 5
Basic materials 6
Dracula 8
Gruesome Gargoyle 10
The Cake Kraken 12
Mean Merlin 14
Vampire Bat 16
Frankie Stein 18
Slime Monster 20
Undead Zombie Ted 22
Evil Clown 24
Yummy Mummy 26
Wicked Witch 28
Freaky Feline 30
Spiky Sea Serpent 32
Arachnophobia 34
Jolly Roger 36
Frightful Phantom 38
Grim Reaper 40
Bag of Bones 42
Spiteful Stinger 44
Creepy Coffin 46

Introduction

Welcome to my world of scary sugarcraft! Many children as well as adults hold a fascination for all things horrible – ghosts, witches, zombies, monsters, things that go bump in the night, things that crawl and sliver – and they are all here, created in sugarpaste to adorn cakes for Halloween, birthday parties or any sort of celebration with a horror theme.

Use the skull and crossbones for a pirate-themed party, or perhaps the vampire, witch or gargoyle on Halloween. The slime monster is perfect for sci-fi fans, and there's even a zombie teddy if you really want to give your guests nightmares.

I have tried to keep the designs as simple as possible with minimal equipment and easily available materials. Although I have used a simple sugar modelling paste, or in some cases just sugarpaste (fondant) with nothing else added, many of the models could be made using different modelling materials such as marzipan, modelling chocolate, Mexican paste or even polymer clay and other non-edible media if a lasting model is preferred.

Edibles

Clear piping gel Use clear piping gel for the 'Slime Monster' (see page 20), or mix with edible green food colouring for 'Undead Zombie Ted' (see page 22).

Red edible food colouring pen

Selection of edible sprinkles Gold, silver and black sugar pearls, and tiny edible stars

Edible metallic paint

Dark brown edible food colour powder

Edible candy sticks These can be either bought or made and dried in advance. Mix 250g (9oz) of sugarpaste or royal icing with half a teaspoon of tylose powder, CMC or gum tragacanth. Roll into thin sausages, cut to short lengths and allow to dry for at least 24 hours, preferably longer.

Note

Some of the models are formed around a food-grade kebab, barbecue or cake-pop stick (for example, Dracula on page 8). These can be stuck directly into a cake as the stick used is food-approved. If you prefer not to use a stick as a support, leave the model to dry for 24 hours and remove the stick by twisting and pulling it out carefully.

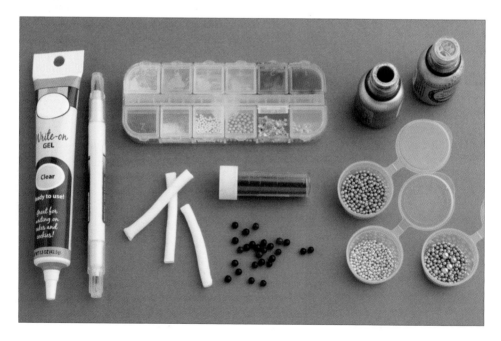

Making simple modelling paste

Add about 1 x 5ml teaspoon of tylose powder, CMC or gum tragacanth to 225g (8oz) of sugarpaste, fondant or ready-to-roll icing. Knead the powder in well and leave for a short time or overnight before using. For smaller amounts, use just a pinch of the powder and knead in as before.

Equipment

Food-grade kebab, barbecue or cake-pop sticks

Multi-mould for hands, ears and wings

Small digital jewellery scales – inexpensive ones are available on internet auction sites

Small, fine palette knife

Ruler

Rolling pin

Cutting wheel

Waterbrushes for painting

Large stitching wheel

Zigzag wheel

Cotton bud

Dusting brush

Fine paintbrush

Smile tool (petal-veining tool or drinking straw)

Dresden tool

Dogbone or ball tool

Small, fine-pointed scissors

Cocktail sticks or toothpicks

Large circle cutter

Small, fine-mesh nylon sieve or tea strainer

Shape cutters – circles, squares, ovals and hearts

Strip cutters

No. 16 (4mm) plain piping tube

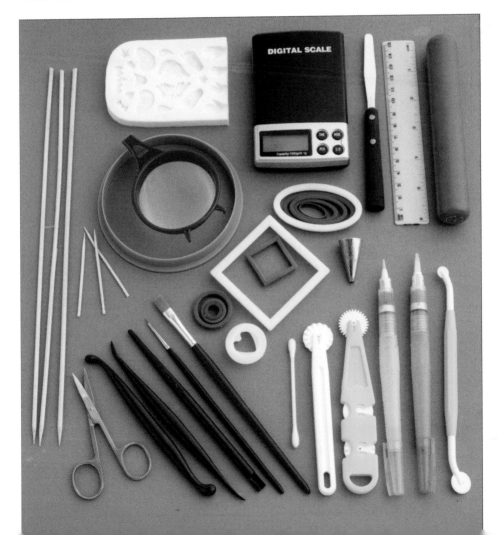

Dracula

Materials:

Small amount of white modelling paste

Red food-colouring pen

50g (1¾oz) black modelling paste

25g (1oz) red modelling paste

Tools:

Rolling pin

2cm (¾in) heart cutter

Dresden tool

Small, fine palette knife

Smile tool (petal-veining tool or drinking straw)

Multi-mould for small hands and pointed ears

Food-grade kebab stick, barbecue stick or cake-pop stick

10cm (4in) circle cutter or template

Ruler

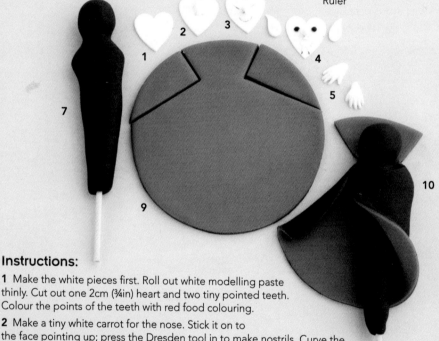

Instructions:

1 Make the white pieces first. Roll out white modelling paste thinly. Cut out one 2cm (¾in) heart and two tiny pointed teeth. Colour the points of the teeth with red food colouring.

2 Make a tiny white carrot for the nose. Stick it on to the face pointing up; press the Dresden tool in to make nostrils. Curve the nose down.

3 Mark the eyes and eyebrows with the end of the small, fine palette knife. Make two tiny black eyes and stick them in place.

4 Mark the mouth with the smile tool. Attach the teeth by pressing them on to the dampened mouth.

5 Make two small, white hands and two white ears from the multi-mould.

6 Keep all the white items covered or in a plastic bag to keep them soft until you are ready to stick them on to the body.

7 For the body, use 25g (1oz) of black modelling paste to make a 10cm (4in) long carrot shape. Push the stick in through the pointed end. Push it up as far as it will go without coming out. Reshape if necessary.

8 Roll between your fingers a short way down from the rounded end to make the neck and shoulders. Pinch the shoulders outwards slightly and gently flatten the chest.

9 For the cape, roll out the black and red modelling paste thinly. Cut out a red 10cm (4in) circle and place it on top of the black paste. Roll again to join the layers. Cut again with the 10cm (4in) circle cutter. Cut right-angles out as shown (you could use a large, square cutter or a knife and ruler).

10 Dampen the back of the neck and body. Lay it on the red side of the cape. Make sure that it sticks to the neck and shoulders. Dampen the edges of the cape to form sleeves. Bring one over the front of the body to the shoulder. Insert a hand under the edge of the cape.

11 Fold over the other edge of the cape and insert the other hand.

12 Flick the front edge of the cape back to reveal the red lining.

13 Stick on the face and ears.

14 Leave to dry until the cape holds its shape.

Gruesome Gargoyle

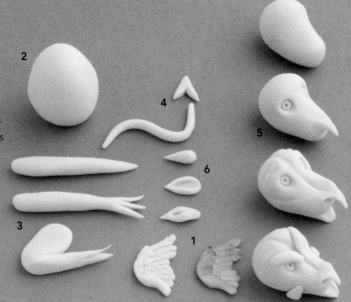

Materials:

50g (1¾oz) stone-coloured
  modelling paste

Dark brown edible food
  colour powder

Tools:

Multi-mould for bird wings

Small, fine-pointed scissors

No. 16 (4mm) piping tube

Cocktail stick

Dresden tool

Dusting brush

Small, fine palette knife

Cutting wheel

Instructions:

1 Make one pair of wings from modelling paste and leave to dry.

2 Make the body by shaping 20g (¾oz) of modelling paste into an egg shape. Stand it upright.

3 For the legs, make four 5cm (2in) long carrots using 2g (¹⁄₁₆oz) for each leg. Use the cutting wheel to cut three claws into the pointed end of each leg. Use the fine palette knife to release the legs from the worksurface as the pointed toes will be delicate. Roll up two of the legs from the fatter end and flatten them slightly. Stick these to the base of the body for the back legs, toes facing forwards. Stick the remaining two legs to the front of the body with the toes bent forwards.

4 Roll a small pea-sized piece of modelling paste out to a thin 6cm (2¼in) sausage for the tail. Shape a tiny piece of paste into a triangle and cut a 'v' into it. Attach the triangle to the end of the tail. Attach the tail to the body.

5 Make a 10g (⅜oz) pear shape for the head. Pinch to make a very pointed nose. Cut the mouth with scissors. Mark the eyes using the piping tube and make a cocktail-stick hole in the middle. Mark the nostrils, wrinkles and mouth with the Dresden tool. Add tiny, thin sausages of paste for the eyebrows and cheeks and stick them in position.

6 Make two ears using two tiny carrot shapes. Flatten them in the middle with the Dresden tool. Pinch the base of each together and stick them on the back of the head.

7 Brush gently with dark brown edible food colour powder all over the body and wings to give the appearance of weathered stone.

8 Attach the wings. Mix a tiny pea-sized piece of modelling paste with a couple of drops of water to make a thick glue. Put a little on each wing and stick them to the back of the body. Prop up the wings if necessary while drying.

Materials:

20g (¾oz) red sugarpaste or marzipan
2 edible black sugar pearls

Tools:

Zigzag wheel
No. 16 (4mm) piping tube

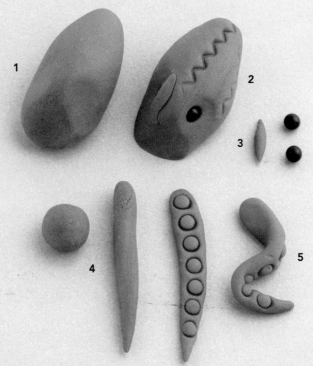

Instructions:

1 For the body, shape 10g (⅜oz) of sugarpaste into an oval. Pinch the sides together at one end, and press that end gently to flatten it slightly.

2 Make two holes for the eyes and insert the black sugar pearls. Mark zigzag lines along the length of the body from behind the eyes.

3 Make two very tiny sausages for the eyelids and attach them over the eyes.

4 Make eight small pea-sized pieces, all the same size, and roll each one to a 15cm (6in) long pointed carrot for the legs. Emboss tentacles along each leg using the plain piping tube.

5 Shape each leg differently by twisting and curling.

6 Flatten and dampen the wide end of each leg. Attach the legs under the front end of the body.

Mean Merlin

Materials:

50g (1¾oz) purple modelling paste

Small piece of flesh-coloured sugarpaste for the face

Small piece of white sugarpaste for the beard, moustache and eyebrows

Clear piping gel

Tiny edible stars

Tools:

Food-grade kebab stick, barbecue stick or cake-pop stick

Rolling pin

1.5cm (½in) circle cutter

Cocktail stick or toothpick

Dresden tool

2.5cm (1in) square cutter

Small nylon-mesh tea strainer or sieve

Small, fine palette knife

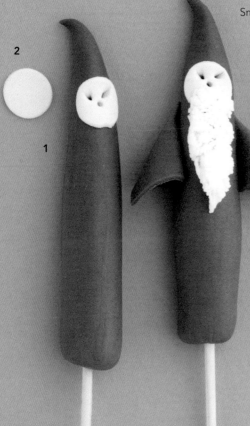

Instructions:

1 Shape 25g (1oz) of purple modelling paste into a 10cm (4in) long pointed carrot. Push the stick into the fat end as far as possible without it coming out at the top.

2 Roll out the flesh-coloured sugarpaste thinly and cut out a 1.5cm (½in) circle. Attach the circle to the purple body as shown. Mark a small hole in the centre for the nose, and press the Dresden tool in for the eyes. Make sure you push through to the purple layer to make the eyes dark.

3 Roll out the purple modelling paste and cut out two 2.5cm (1in) squares. Fold over each square diagonally to form triangles.

4 For each triangle, press one edge together and leave the other edge open for the sleeve. Dampen along the pressed edge and attach the sleeves to the sides of the body.

5 Press white sugarpaste through the tea strainer or sieve for the beard. Cut the 'fluff' off in one piece if possible, using the small, fine palette knife. Dampen the body where the beard will go and attach it, pressing it into place with the cocktail stick or toothpick to avoid flattening it.

6 Make four tiny teardrop shapes from the white sugarpaste, and attach two for the moustache and two for the eyebrows.

7 Make a tiny nose from flesh-coloured sugarpaste. Stick it in place.

8 Dot piping gel over the pointed hat. Use a cocktail stick or toothpick dampened with a little of the piping gel to pick up tiny edible stars and attach them to the dots of gel on the hat.

Vampire Bat

Materials:

10g (⅜oz) black modelling paste

Tiny piece of white sugarpaste for
the teeth

Tools:

Greaseproof paper or baking parchment

Wing template

Rolling pin

Dresden tool

Cutting wheel

Palette knife

Instructions:

1 Trace over and cut out a template for the
wings using greaseproof paper or
baking parchment.

2 Roll out black modelling paste thinly. Cut
around the wing template. Mark lines for the
wings as shown using a knife or Dresden tool.

3 For the body, shape a small 2g (¹⁄₁₆oz) pea of
black modelling paste into a 2cm (¾in) sausage. Shape the face
forward to a point.

4 Pinch the ears up from the sides of the head.

5 Mark the eyes and nostrils with the Dresden tool. Mark the mouth
with a knife.

6 Roll out the white sugarpaste very thinly and cut out two tiny
triangles for the teeth. Stick them in place.

7 Alternatively, if you have any royal icing or buttercream already
made, pipe the teeth on using a fine piping tube. You could even
paint the teeth on using white edible food colour.

8 Stick the body to the wings.

*The bat can be used flat on cakes straight
away or, if left to dry until hard, it could be
stuck on the edge of a cake to look as if
it is flying.*

Frankie Stein

Materials:

10g (⅜oz) pale green
   modelling paste

2 edible black sugar pearls

40g (1½oz) black
   modelling paste

2 edible silver sugar pearls

Tools:

Dresden tool

Multi-mould for large hands

Ball tool

Small, fine palette knife

Six-petal flower cutter

Food-grade kebab stick,
   barbecue stick or
   cake-pop stick

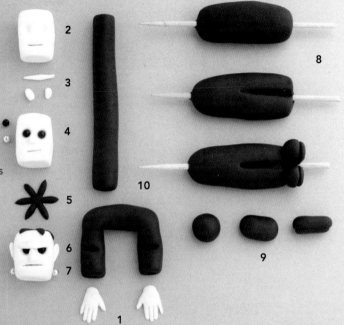

Instructions:

1 Use the Dresden tool to push a small, pea-sized piece of pale green modelling paste into each of the large hands on the mould. Take the hands out of the mould straight away and leave to dry for a short time.

2 For the head, shape 10g (⅜oz) of pale green modelling paste to form an oblong 2.5 x1.5cm (1 x ½in). Sharpen the edges by pinching them. Mark the eye sockets with the ball tool and mark the mouth with the knife.

3 Make a tiny sausage of pale green modelling paste, 1.5cm (½in) long, for a single eyebrow. Make two tiny, green balls for the ears.

4 Insert black sugar pearls in the eye sockets for the eyes. Shape a tiny triangle for the nose. Stick it in the centre of the face.

5 Roll out the black modelling paste thinly. Cut out a six-petal flower and stick it on top of the head for hair.

6 Stick the single eyebrow in place, shading the tops of the eyes. Dampen the sides of the head in line with the nose and stick on the ears. Press them in the middle with the Dresden tool.

7 Mark a hole on each side of the head for the neck bolts. Dampen and insert the silver sugar pearls.

8 For the body and legs, shape 20g (¾oz) of black modelling paste into a 5cm (2in) sausage. Insert the stick right through. Mark the legs with the Dresden tool or a knife.

9 Make two 2g (¹⁄₁₆oz) pea-sizes of black modelling paste for the boots. Shape them to make small ovals. Mark around the soles with a knife and attach them under the legs.

10 For the arms, shape 15g (½oz) of black modelling paste into a 10cm (4in) sausage. Bend to form the angles as shown, pinching the corners to make the shoulders. Make a hole in each end for the hands. Press the knife or the Dresden tool in half-way down each arm for the elbows. Bend the arms forward from the elbows.

11 Dampen the top of the body. Place the arms on the stick and push them down to join on to the body. Press a hollow in the front centre of the arms for the head. Dampen the hollow and attach the head.

12 Dampen the ends of the hands and attach them to the arms.

13 Allow to dry, lying the model down until the head is secure.

Slime Monster

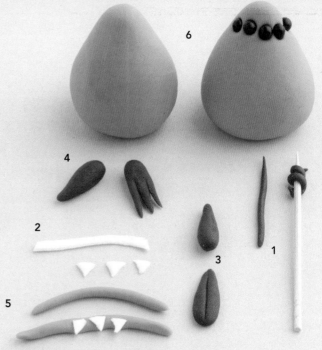

Materials:

Small amounts of red and white modelling paste

25g (1oz) green modelling paste

5 edible black sugar pearls

Clear piping gel

1 edible silver sugar pearl

Tools:

Cocktail stick

Palette knife

Instructions:

1 Roll a very thin pointed sausage of red modelling paste about 4cm (1½in) long. Twirl it around a cocktail stick and leave to set.

2 Roll the white modelling paste thinly. Cut tiny triangles for the teeth.

3 For the tongue, shape a small pea of red modelling paste into a short carrot shape. Flatten, and mark a line down the centre.

4 Shape two small peas of red sugarpaste into short carrot shapes for the feet. Cut into the pointed ends to make three pointed toes.

5 Roll two thin sausages of green modelling paste each 4cm (1½in) long for the lips. Stick the teeth on to one of the green sausages and turn it over so that the teeth are underneath. Join the two lips together at the ends.

6 Shape the rest of the green modelling paste into an egg shape. Make one hole in the top for the spiral, and five holes for the eyes. Dampen the eye holes and push in the black sugar pearls for eyes.

7 Dampen the backs of the lips and stick them to the front of the face.

8 Attach the feet under the body.

9 Dampen and attach the tongue.

10 Dampen the top hole and attach the twirled red paste. Put a tiny dot of piping gel on the point and stick on the silver ball.

11 Squeeze a large blob of piping gel on the tip of the tongue.

Undead Zombie Ted

Materials:

60g (2oz) grey modelling paste

Small amounts of red and white modelling paste

Edible black sugar pearls

Small amount of piping gel mixed with edible green food colour

Tools:

Small, fine palette knife

Dresden tool

Rolling pin

3cm (1¼in) oval cutter

Stitching wheel

Cocktail stick

Smile tool (petal-veining tool or drinking straw)

Dogbone or ball tool

Fine-pointed scissors

Small piping bag

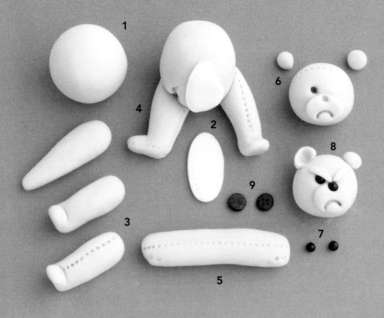

Instructions:

1 Shape an oval with 25g (1oz) of grey modelling paste. Mark a rip up from one side with the Dresden tool.

2 Roll out white sugarpaste thinly for the tummy. Cut out the oval, stitch round the edge using the stitching wheel and stick the tummy on to the body. Use the fine palette knife to release the tummy from the worksurface. Leave one edge unstuck to add green slime later.

3 For the legs, shape two 5g (¼oz) pieces of grey modelling paste into 4cm (1½in) carrots. Turn up the pointed ends for the feet. Stitch around each foot and up the leg using the stitching wheel.

4 Stick the legs on to the body, with one hanging off at an angle.

5 For the arms, shape 10g (⅜oz) of grey modelling paste into a 6cm (2¼in) sausage. Stitch along the whole arm using the stitching wheel and use a cocktail stick to mark the stitching for the paws. Attach the arms on top of the body.

6 Shape 10g (⅜oz) of grey modelling paste into a ball for the head. Stitch around it using the stitching wheel. Attach a tiny oval of grey modelling paste for the muzzle. Mark a sad mouth with the smile tool or drinking straw. Make a small indentation for the nose and eyes. For the ears, make two tiny balls of grey modelling paste.

7 Insert one black sugar pearl for the nose, and one for an eye. Shape two tiny sausages for the frowning eyebrows.

8 Attach the ears to the top of the head. Push each ear into the head with the dogbone or ball tool, supporting the back of the ear with your finger. This will cup and curve the ears. Cut a nick in one ear with fine-pointed scissors.

9 Shape a tiny piece of red sugarpaste into a ball to make a button. Flatten it with your finger and mark buttonholes with a cocktail stick. Attach the button to the face for the second eye.

10 Put some green piping gel in a small piping bag. Cut a small hole or use a small, plain piping tube. Pipe oozing green slime in various places.

Evil Clown

Materials:

20g (¾oz) white sugarpaste

Small amounts of red, black, yellow, green and orange sugarpaste (or any other mix of colours)

Edible red sugar pearls

Tools:

Dresden tool

Rolling pin

2cm (¾in) oval cutter

Fine-mesh nylon sieve or tea strainer

Small, fine palette knife

Instructions:

1 Make two tiny ovals of white sugarpaste for the ears.

2 Roll the rest of the white paste into a ball for the head, then roll your finger across one end to make a pear shape.

3 Make a hole in the centre for the nose.

4 Attach the ears in line with the nose by pressing each oval into the head with the Dresden tool.

5 Make a small red ball of sugarpaste for the nose. Attach it to the face.

6 Roll out some red paste thinly. for the lips. Cut a 2cm (¾in) oval and curve the ends up slightly.

7 Roll out the black sugarpaste thinly. Cut out two 2cm (¾in) ovals. Cut each one with the edge of the oval cutter again to look like horns.

8 Attach the lips under the nose. Use the Dresden tool to mark the mouth from side to side. Attach the black horn shapes to the face.

9 Make holes for the eyes and insert red sugar pearls or red paste shaped into two pea-sized balls.

10 Choose the three colours for the hair. Press the sugarpaste through the tea strainer in any order you choose; I put yellow through first, followed by green and then orange. Use the palette knife to cut the hair off the back of the tea strainer when it is the chosen length. Carefully divide it in two and stick above the ears.

24

Yummy Mummy

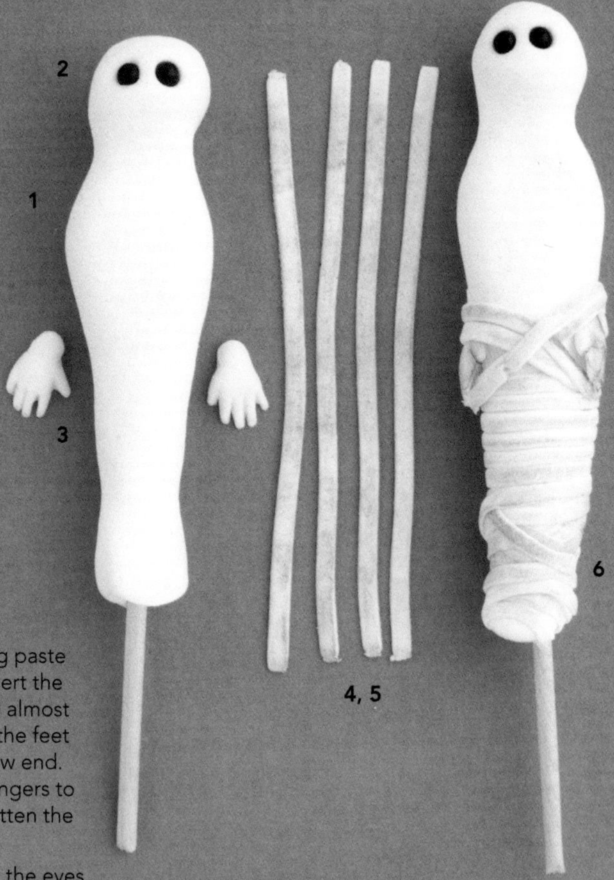

Materials:

40g (1½oz) white or cream modelling paste

Edible black sugar pearls

Dark brown edible food colour powder

Tools:

Food-grade kebab stick, barbecue stick or cake-pop stick

Multi-mould for small hands

Rolling pin

Music-stave or fine-strip cutter

Dusting brush

Instructions:

1 Make 25g (1oz) of the modelling paste into a 9cm (3½in) carrot shape. Insert the stick through from the narrow end almost up to the top of the head. Shape the feet by pinching the paste at the narrow end. Roll the wide end between your fingers to make the shoulders and head. Flatten the chest slightly.

2 Insert the black sugar pearls for the eyes.

3 Use the Dresden tool to push a small pea-sized piece of white modelling paste into each of the small hands on the mould. Stick the hands to the sides of the body.

4 Roll out the rest of the white modelling paste thinly. Cut out sugar strips using the music-stave or fine-strip cutter.

5 Brush the strips gently with the dark brown edible food colour powder.

6 Dampen the body and wrap the strips around the body. Hold the body by the stick while you are doing this. Continue adding strips until the body and head are covered, but leave the hands and eyes peering through.

7 Brush the hands, feet and anywhere else that needs extra colour with the dark brown.

8 Allow to set before removing the support stick.

26

Wicked Witch

Materials:

25g (1oz) black modelling paste

Small amounts of pale green and orange sugarpaste

Tools:

Rolling pin

2.5cm (1in) and 1cm (½in) circle cutters

Small, fine palette knife

Food-grade kebab stick, barbecue stick or cake-pop stick 2cm (¾in) oval cutter

Fine-mesh nylon sieve or tea strainer

Dresden tool

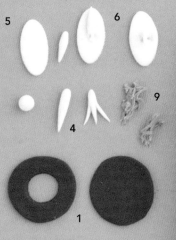

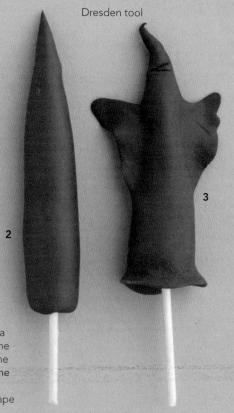

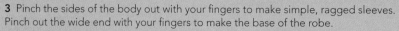

Instructions:

1 Roll out a small amount of the black modelling paste thinly. Cut out a 2.5cm (1in) circle and cut the centre out with the 1cm (½in) circle cutter.

2 Shape the rest of the black modelling paste into a 10cm (4in) long pointed carrot. Push the stick into the fat end as far as possible without it coming out at the top. Make sure that the 1cm (½in) cutter fits down the cone, as the black circle will form the rim of the hat. Mark a few lines on the hat part with a knife and shape it to look crooked.

3 Pinch the sides of the body out with your fingers to make simple, ragged sleeves. Pinch out the wide end with your fingers to make the base of the robe.

4 Make two tiny cones of pale green sugarpaste for the hands. Cut into the pointed end to make at least three sharp-pointed fingers. Dampen the ends of the sleeves and attach the hands. Curve the sleeves over the ends of the hands.

5 Roll out the pale green sugarpaste thinly. Cut a 2cm (¾in) oval.

6 Make a very tiny carrot of pale green sugarpaste – half the length of the face. Stick it on the centre of the oval. Press the fat end with the Dresden tool to make nostrils. Curve the nose over to form a hooked nose.

7 Put the hat rim in place and dampen it slightly on the inner rim to secure it.

8 Dampen the back of the face and stick it under the rim of the hat. Use the wide end of the Dresden tool to push a mouth in, and the narrow end to mark the eyes. Make sure that you push the tool far enough into the black paste underneath to look dark.

9 Push a little orange paste through a fine-mesh nylon sieve or tea strainer to make fluff. Dampen around the face and attach the hair.

10 Leave to dry overnight.

Freaky Feline

Materials:

20g (¾oz) black modelling paste

10g (⅜oz) sugarpaste ball wrapped in plastic food wrap (Clingfilm) for support

Small amounts of red and white modelling paste

Tools:

Small, fine palette knife

Cocktail stick or toothpick

Dresden tool

Rolling pin

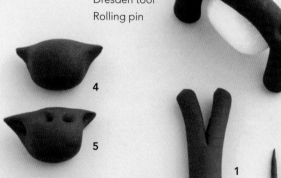

Instructions:

1 Shape 10g (⅜oz) of the black modelling paste into a 10cm (4in) sausage.

2 Make a 3cm (1¼in) cut into each end. Separate the legs and curve the body into a 'c' shape. Stand the body up on its feet. Make a slight hollow with your finger where the head will go. Make a small vertical indentation where the tail will go. Support the body with the wrapped ball of sugarpaste until the body is dry (at least 24 hours).

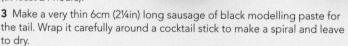

3 Make a very thin 6cm (2¼in) long sausage of black modelling paste for the tail. Wrap it carefully around a cocktail stick to make a spiral and leave to dry.

4 For the head, shape 5g (¼oz) of black modelling paste into an oval. Pinch out the ears to point out flat, level with the top edge of the head. This will make the cat look angry. Press into each ear with the Dresden tool to make a hollow.

5 Use the Dresden tool to make hollows for the eye sockets too.

6 Cut two tiny, pointed teeth from rolled-out white modelling paste and stick them on the lower half of the head.

7 For the eyes, make a very tiny ball of red modelling paste and attach a sliver of black straight across it. Cut straight across the middle of the black line to make two pointed, oval eyes. Dampen the eye sockets and stick in the eyes.

8 Make two tiny sausages of black modelling paste and stick them on as eyebrows to make the cat frown.

9 Shape two tiny ovals of black for the cheeks. Stick them on, making sure the teeth show.

10 Add a tiny black ball for the nose.

11 Mash together a small, pea-sized piece of black modelling paste with a couple of drops of water until they form a thick, stringy glue. Use a very small amount to stick the head and tail on to the body.

Spiky Sea Serpent

Materials:

Tiny amount of white modelling paste

10g (⅜oz) purple modelling paste

Edible black sugar pearls

10g (⅜oz) ball of sugarpaste wrapped in plastic food wrap (Clingfilm) for support

Clear piping gel

Edible silver sugar pearls

Tools:

Rolling pin

Small, fine palette knife or cutting wheel

Sharp-pointed scissors

Dresden tool

Cocktail stick or toothpick

Instructions:

1 Roll out the tiny amount of white sugarpaste thinly. Cut two very thin, pointed teeth. Curve the teeth and leave them to dry.

2 Make two tiny purple sausages for the eyelids.

3 Shape the rest of the purple modelling paste into a 10cm (4in) pointed sausage. Cut a mouth with the scissors.

4 Use the scissors to cut spikes. Keep the scissors very flat and close to the surface of the paste to make the points nice and sharp. Start at the head end and cut the spikes down the back first, then cut one row of spikes down each side.

5 Make holes for the eyes with the Dresden tool. Dampen the eye sockets and stick in the black sugar pearls for eyes.

6 Stick on the eyelids, pointing down at the front to make the serpent look angry.

7 Curve the body round and up. Rest the head on the support and leave to dry. Make sure that the spikes are sticking up where possible.

8 Put a tiny dot of piping gel on the tip of each spike along the top of the serpent. Attach a tiny silver ball to the tip of each spine. Dip the tip of a cocktail stick into piping gel – just enough to make it tacky – and use this to pick up each silver ball.

9 Dampen the top of the inside of the mouth and attach the tiny, white teeth, pointing downwards.

Arachnophobia

Materials:

12.5g (⁷⁄₁₆oz) black modelling paste
10g (⅜oz) red modelling paste
Black edible food colour powder
Edible black sugar pearls

Tools:

Dresden tool
Dusting brush
Small, fine palette knife

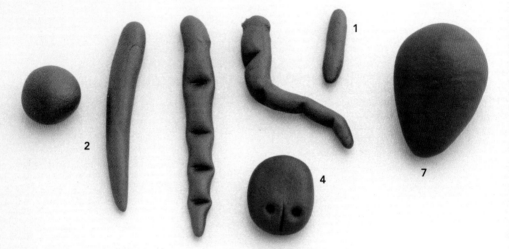

Instructions:

1 For the jaws, shape two very small, pea-sized pieces of red modelling paste into 2cm (¾in) sausages. Press in three indentations using the Dresden tool down the length of each sausage without cutting through.

2 Make eight large, pea-sized pieces of red modelling paste, all the same size, for the legs. Roll each leg into a thin, pointed 5cm (2in) carrot shape. Press in four indentations using the Dresden tool down the length of each one without cutting through. Curve each leg and bend out each foot. Press the rounded end gently to flatten it slightly.

3 Brush gently across each joint of the legs and the jaws with black edible food colour powder.

4 For the head, shape 2.5g (⅛oz) of black modelling paste into a ball. Make two holes for the eyes, dampen the eye sockets and attach the black sugar pearls. Mark hairs along the head with the knife .

5 Attach the jaws at the front of the head, under the eyes.

6 Dampen each leg at the flattened end and attach four down each side of the body, making sure the legs are curved with the feet pointing out.

7 Shape 10g (⅜oz) of black modelling paste into an egg shape to make the abdomen. Mark hairs along the abdomen with the knife. Dampen the narrow end and attach it to the back of the head.

Jolly Roger

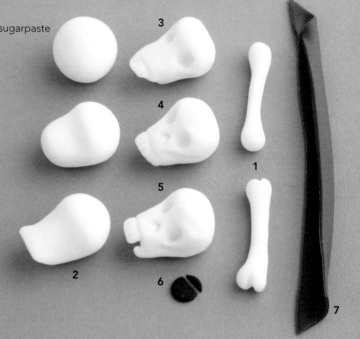

Materials:

15g (½oz) white or cream sugarpaste

Small amounts of red and black modelling paste

Edible dark brown food colour powder

Edible gold paint

Tools:

Dresden tool

Small, fine palette knife

Fine-pointed scissors

Dusting brush

Dogbone or ball tool

Rolling pin

1cm (½in) circle cutter

Cutting wheel

Fine paintbrush

Instructions:

1 Make two large pea shapes of white sugarpaste for the bones. Roll in the middle of each one to make a long bone shape with rounded ends. Using the Dresden tool, rock over the ends to shape them. Lay the bones over each other to make the crossbones. Dampen between the bones where they touch to stick them together.

2 For the skull, shape a 10g (⅜oz) ball of white sugarpaste into a pear shape by rolling it at one end. Pinch into the thin, narrow end for teeth. Mark the teeth with the knife. Cut out one tooth with fine-pointed scissors.

3 Mark the eyeballs with the dogbone or ball tool.

4 Mark the nose with the Dresden tool.

5 Mark the sides of the skull and above the eyes with the Dresden tool.

6 Roll out the black paste thinly for the eye patch. Cut out a 1cm (½in) circle. Cut off a small piece. Dampen the back of the eye patch and lay it over one eye.

7 Roll out the red modelling paste thinly for the bandana. Cut a strip approximately 15 x 2cm (6 x ¾in) and cut each end to a point. Fold the strip over along its length and wrap it around the skull. Pinch together at the join as if it is tied.

8 Dampen the top of the crossbones and lay the skull on top.

9 Dust all over gently with edible dark brown food colour powder, including the bandana, to age it. Use the fine paintbrush to darken in the eye socket and other indentations.

10 Paint one tooth with edible gold paint.

Frightful Phantom

Materials:

20g (¾oz) white modelling paste
5cm (2in) white edible candy stick
Edible black sugar pearls

Tools:

10cm (4in) circle cutter or small plate
Rolling pin
Dresden tool
Dogbone or ball tool
Small, fine palette knife

Instructions:

1 Attach a small ball of white modelling paste to the top of an edible candy stick. You could use a small, soft sweet, such as a small marshmallow, instead.

2 Roll out the rest of the white modelling paste thinly. Allow it to dry slightly on each side. Cut out a 10cm (4in) circle. A fine palette knife will help when releasing the circle from the worksurface. Lay the candy stick in the middle of the circle with the ball in the middle. Fold the circle over it.

3 Hold the stick up, off the worksurface, and press the paste to side of the ball, making folds.

4 Bring up the sides to form arms. Pinch the paste in under the arms.

5 Mark the open mouth with the wide end of the Dresden tool.

6 Make the eye sockets with the dogbone or ball tool and insert edible black pearls for eyes. Mark eyebrows with the end of the fine palette knife.

7 Lay the model down and allow it to dry.

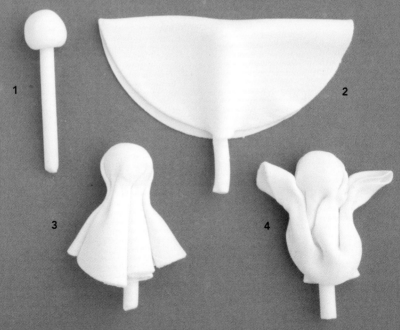

Grim Reaper

Materials:

Small amount of white modelling paste
Edible silver paint
20g (¾oz) black modelling paste

Tools:

Rolling pin
3cm (1¼in) oval cutter
Paintbrush
5cm (2in) oval cutter
6.5cm (2½in) oval cutter
Cocktail stick or toothpick

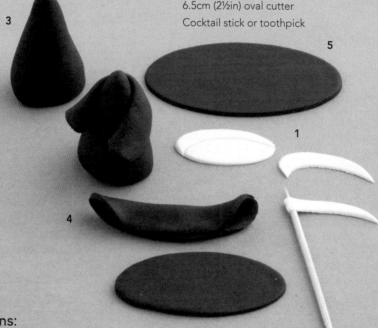

Instructions:

1 Make the scythe first to give it time to dry. Roll out the white modelling paste thinly. Cut a 3cm (1¼in) oval, and use the same cutter to cut again for the blade, as shown. Roll the fatter end around the end of the cocktail stick. Lay it flat on the surface and allow to dry, turning it over a couple of times to dry evenly on both sides.

2 When dry, paint the scythe with edible silver paint.

3 For the body, shape 10g (⅜oz) of the black paste into a 4cm (1½in) cone.

4 Roll out the rest of the black modelling paste thinly to make the sleeves and the robe. Cut out a 5cm (2in) oval and fold it in half lengthways. Attach it to the cone as shown to form the sleeves.

5 Cut out a 6.5cm (2½in) oval from the rolled-out black paste. Lay it over the body, draping it higher than the head. Shape the top into a deep hood so that you cannot see inside.

6 Attach the scythe over one arm. Dampen the cocktail stick if necessary to hold it in place.

Bag of Bones

Materials:

40g (1½oz) black modelling paste
20g (¾oz) white modelling paste
Edible black sugar pearls

Tools:

Plastic bag or bowl to cover items to keep
   them soft
Multi-mould for small hands
Dresden tool
Small, fine palette knife
Dogbone or ball tool

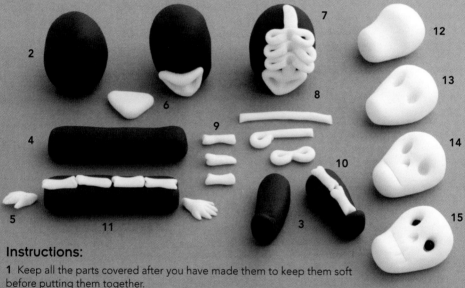

Instructions:

1 Keep all the parts covered after you have made them to keep them soft
before putting them together.

2 Shape 20g (¾oz) of the black modelling paste into an oval for the body.

3 Make two 5g (¼oz) carrot-shaped legs. Bend up the narrow end of each
one for the feet.

4 Form one 10g (⅜oz) black sausage 5cm (2in) long for the arms. Make an
indentation in each end to hold the hands.

5 Make two hands from the white paste in the multi-mould.

6 Form a pea-sized piece of white paste into a triangle. Press this on to
the body for the hips. Press the wide end of the Dresden tool deeply into
the triangle for the hollow parts so that the dark paste shows through.

7 Form a 3cm (1¼in) thin sausage of white modelling paste for the spine.
Attach it to the front of the body above the hips.

8 Make a long thin sausage of white paste for the ribs. Cut three 4cm
(1½in) lengths. Loop each end of each rib into the middle. Dampen the
spine and stick each rib on to the spine. Press them on to the spine with
the wide end of the Dresden tool.

9 Make eight very small, white bones, each 1cm (½in) long. Thin the middle by rolling, and make an indentation at each end using the Dresden tool. Keep the bones covered.

10 Stick two bones down each leg. Attach the legs to the body.

11 Stick four bones end-to-end along the arm. Dampen holes at the ends of the arms and stick in the hands. Dampen the top of the body and press the arms on with the bones facing forwards. Press a dip in the middle of the arms at the top with your finger for the head to go. Position the arms and hands. This body with arms and legs no longer needs to be covered.

12 For the skull, shape a 10g (⅖oz) ball of white modelling paste into a pear shape by rolling one end with your finger.

13 Mark the eyeballs with the dogbone or ball tool.

14 Mark the nose with the Dresden tool.

15 Mark the teeth with the knife. Dampen the sockets and press in edible black sugar pearls for the eyes.

16 Dampen the indentation on the top of the arms and attach the head.

Spiteful Stinger

Materials:

5g (⅕oz) black modelling paste

Edible red sugar pearls or red
  modelling paste

Tools:

Small, fine palette knife

Dresden tool

Instructions:

1 Roll 1g (¹⁄₃₂oz) of black modelling paste into a 5cm (2in) carrot shape for the tail. Carefully press horizontal lines along its length with a knife, without cutting through. Curve the tail, with the segments facing inwards, into a 'c' shape. Press the pointed end to form the sting. Leave to dry.

2 For the pincers, shape four tiny, curved teardrop shapes, two small and two slightly smaller. Flatten them slightly. Attach the two different sizes with the points facing for each pincer. Make two 2cm (¾in) thin sausages for the 'arms'. Mark the segments as before. Attach the pincers at the ends of the 'arms'.

3 Make the body by shaping 1g (¹⁄₃₂oz) of black modelling paste into pointed oval. Press the knife in to make segments as shown. Make indentations for the eyes, dampen the sockets and insert the red sugar pearls for eyes. Dampen the ends of the 'arms' and attach them, facing forwards, under the eyes.

4 Roll a very thin, pointed carrot shape 3cm (1¼in) long to make a leg. Carefully press in segments with the Dresden tool or knife. Attach the leg to the side of the body, curving it and pointing the feet outwards. Make eight legs in total and attach each one as you make it. The legs are fragile, so be very careful.

5 Mash a small pea-sized piece of black modelling paste with a couple of drops of water until it forms a thick, stringy glue. Use a very small amount to stick the dry tail under the end of the body with the sting curving over the body. Support it in position if necessary while drying.

Creepy Coffin

Materials:
50g (1¾oz) black modelling paste
Small amount of pale green modelling paste
Dark brown edible food colour powder
Edible gold sugar pearls
Clear piping gel

Tools:
Template for the coffin lid
Greaseproof paper or baking parchment
Rolling pin
Cutting wheel
Multi-mould for large hands
Dusting brush

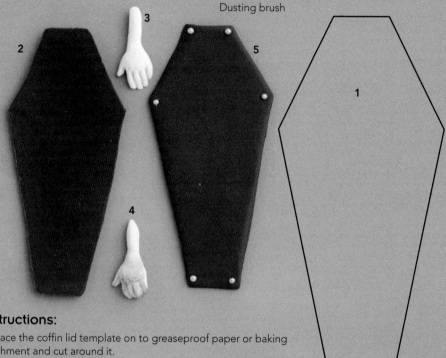

Instructions:

1 Trace the coffin lid template on to greaseproof paper or baking parchment and cut around it.

2 Roll out the black modelling paste. Cut out the coffin lid using the template. Mark holes on the corners. Allow the lid to dry on both sides.

3 Make two large, pale green hands using the multi-mould, with extra paste left on for the wrists. Shape the hands by curving them inwards.

4 Brush the hands gently with dark brown edible food colour powder.

5 Attach edible gold sugar pearls on the marked corners of the lid using a tiny amount of piping gel in each hole. If you want a shiny lid, brush a very thin layer of clear piping gel over the surface.

6 Position the lid and hands on your cake. Mash up a small pea-sized piece of black modelling paste with a couple of drops of water until it forms a thick, stringy glue. Use a very small amount to stick the lid and hands to the cake surface.

Acknowledgements

Special thanks to my editor at Search Press, Katie French; to the photographer, Vanessa Davies; and everyone else at Search Press who was involved in the publication of this book.

You are invited to visit the author's website:
www.franklysweet.co.uk

Publishers' Note

If you would like more books about sugarcraft, try the following books by the same author, all published by Search Press:
Twenty to Make Sugar Animals
Twenty to Make Sugar Birds
Twenty to Make Sugar Fairies
Sensational Sugar Animals